Birthright

Birthright

Poems by

Erika Dreifus

For Andree,

Wishing you
lots of luck with
your poems!

—Erika Dreifus

Kelsay Books

Cover design by Shay Culligan

Author photograph by Jody Christopherson

Cover image provided by Mohamed Hassan via Pixabay.com

(Kelsay Books / Aldrich Press)

ISBN: 978-1-950462-15-5

Kelsay Books Inc.

kelsaybooks.com

502 S 1040 E, A119
American Fork, Utah 84003

For My Parents

Acknowledgments

I am grateful to the editors of the publications in which these poems, some in earlier versions, first appeared.

929: "Complicity," "Miriam, Quarantined"
Adanna: "Umbilicus"
Alyss: "Wherever You've Gone, Joe DiMaggio"
American Journal of Nursing: "The Autumn of H1N1"
Babel Fruit: "Thirteen Ways of Looking at My Latest Cold"
Christian Science Monitor: "Meteorology"
Forward: "Family Plots" (as "Mount Zion"), "September 1, 1946"
Haaretz: "Ode to a Rescuer"
Hevria: "Black Sheep in the World to Come"
The Hollins Critic: "Fighting Words"
Jewcy: "Birthright," "Sabbath Rest 2.0"
Jewess: "The Book of Vashti"
Jewish Currents: "Aftermath" (2017/5778 Jewish New Year supplement)
Jewish Journal: "The O-Word," "Pharaoh's Daughter Addresses Linda Sarsour," "This Woman's Prayer"
Lilith: "Dinah Speaks" (as "A Poem for Vayishlach"), "*Kaddish* for My Uterus"
Medical Journal of Australia: "Homage to My Skull"
MissouriReview.com: "Jerusalem Dream"
Moment Magazine: "Abel's Brother Anticipates Lady Macbeth: A Soliloquy," "*Dayenu,*" "On Reading Chapter 19 in the Book of Judges," "*Pünktlichkeit*"
New Vilna Review: "Diaspora: A Prose Poem," "Mannheim," "Sisters, or Double *Chai*"
qartsilunni: "With or Without"
ReformJudaism.org: "Questions for the Critics," "Unsolved Mysteries of Samson and Delilah"
Rhyme On Poetry Contest 2018 e-book: "When Your Niece Attends a Jewish Day School"
Silver Birch Press: "Self-Portrait with Root Rescue™"

The Sunlight Press: "Hypothetical Life," "On Refinding My First
  Crush on Facebook," "The Smell of Infection"
Tablet: "The Awakening," "The First Night," "Ruth's Regret"
Theories of Her (anthology): "Vocabulary Lesson, 1977," "We Are
  All Bag Ladies"
Whale Road Review: "The End of the Lines"
The Wild Word: "A Walker in the Post-Blizzard City"
Writing the Words: "My Mother's Olivetti"
Yale Journal for Humanities in Medicine: "Solar Damage"

Additional appreciation goes to the Loudoun County (Va.) Public
Library for selecting "When Your Niece Attends a Jewish Day
School" for honorable mention (free verse) in the 2018 Rhyme On
Poetry Contest; *Whale Road Review* for nominating "The End of
the Lines" for a Pushcart Prize; Manhattan Jewish Experience and
judge Yehoshua November for selecting "Comforts of Home" as
winner of the 2017 Poetry Contest; and Reesa Grushka, whose
Missouri Review essay "Arieh" sourced the composition of
"Jerusalem Dream," which was recognized with honorable
mention by the 2012 "Art of Omission" contest from *The Missouri
Review*/textBOX.

And, of course, I'm immensely thankful to publisher Karen Kelsay
and the Kelsay Books team for welcoming my manuscript and
giving it such a lovely home.

In many ways, *Birthright* has been a lifetime work-in-progress. But
more technically speaking, work on these poems began in 2007;
the book that you're reading now developed over 12 years thanks
to direct instruction and inspiration from the following: the
Achayot (especially, above and beyond, Sivan Rotholz, Talia Liben
Yarmush, and Suzanne Reisman); Amy Gottlieb's "Jewish Sources,
Literary Narrative" classes at Drisha Institute (New York);
Matthew Lippman's online poetry-writing classes with Gotham
Writers Workshop; Sage Cohen's online "Poetry for the People"
courses; Kathleen Graber's Poetry Manuscript workshop at the
Vermont College of Fine Arts Postgraduate Writers Conference;
Wendy Zierler's class on "The Secular Israeli Religious

~Also by Erika Dreifus~

Quiet Americans: Stories

Birthright

Poems by

Erika Dreifus

For Andrec,
wishing you
lots of luck with
your poems!

—Erika Dreifus

Kelsay Books

Cover design by Shay Culligan

Author photograph by Jody Christopherson

Cover image provided by Mohamed Hassan via Pixabay.com

(Kelsay Books / Aldrich Press)

ISBN: 978-1-950462-15-5

Kelsay Books Inc.

kelsaybooks.com

502 S 1040 E, A119
American Fork, Utah 84003

For My Parents

Renaissance: Israeli Poetry and Prayer" at Park Avenue Synagogue (New York); and a session led by Cheryl Pallant that I had the opportunity to sit in on when I was guest faculty at the Red Earth MFA program in Oklahoma City. (Looking back to my own MFA experience some years prior to 2007, I remain grateful to several faculty poets from that time—most of all, Richard Chess—for treating this aspiring fictionist so kindly and helping me begin to grasp the power and potential of poetry.)

Perhaps not coincidentally, 2007 is also the year that brought me back to the city of my birth and marked the beginning of my employment at The City University of New York (CUNY). During the seven years that I remained on staff at the central office, I had the good fortune to work alongside many wonderful colleagues who showed interest in my writing; I connected, too, with a number of exemplary, encouraging poets and other writers across the CUNY campuses. Since my return to New York I've also been lucky to engage with the intellectually enriching communities of the Jewish Book Council and the New York Society Library, among others.

Birthright simply would not exist without the loving, generous presence of too many friends, family members, and assorted champions to name. I thank you all—and I hope that somehow, somewhere, the dear ones already in the world to come are watching this book make its way into this one.

Finally, a concluding shout-out to Sefaria (Sefaria.org), a source for many of the biblical citations/translations that appear throughout this collection. "For the Jewish people," the site explains, "our texts are our collective inheritance." You might even say that they are our birthright.

Contents

Pünktlichkeit	17
Birthright	19
Homage to My Skull	20
Umbilicus	21
Out to Lunch	22
Kaddish for My Uterus	23
This Woman's Prayer	25
We Are All Bag Ladies	26
September 1, 1946	27
Meteorology	28
A Walker in the Post-Blizzard City	29
The Book of Vashti	30
Vocabulary Lesson, 1977	31
Ode to a Rescuer	32
Jerusalem Dream	33
Mannheim	34
Comforts of Home	35
Hypothetical Life	36
The First Night	37
On Refinding My First Crush on Facebook	38
The O-Word	39
Sabbath Rest 2.0	40
Bloodlines	41
Solar Damage	42
The Smell of Infection	44
The Price of Lilith's Freedom	45
Unsolved Mysteries of Samson and Delilah	46
The Autumn of H1N1	47
Ruth's Regret	49
Self-Portrait with Root Rescue™	50
My Mother's Olivetti	51
Dinah Speaks	52
Family Plots	53
Miriam, Quarantined	55

Questions for the Critics   56
The Awakening   57
Sisters, or Double *Chai*   58
Abel's Brother Anticipates Lady Macbeth: A Soliloquy   60
Diaspora: A Prose Poem   61
Aftermath   62
Complicity   63
The End of the Lines   64
The Plot of *Madame Bovary* in 55 Words   65
Fighting Words   66
Thirteen Ways of Looking at My Latest Cold   67
On Reading Chapter 19 in the Book of Judges   70
Wherever You've Gone, Joe DiMaggio   71
Dayenu   72
Pharaoh's Daughter Addresses Linda Sarsour   73
Over the Edge   74
Black Sheep in the World to Come   75
When Your Niece Attends a Jewish Day School   79
A Single Woman of Valor   80
With or Without   82

Pünktlichkeit

with thanks to Steven M. Lowenstein

My father's parents were Germans,
and they were Jews,
and they were born long ago,
one just before and one just after
the outbreak of the war
that was to end all wars,
but didn't.

They came to New York in '37 and '38,
met and married and had a son.
From them, I have inherited
copies of *Der Struwwelpeter*
and *Buddenbrooks,*
a fondness for Riesling,
and *pünktlichkeit.*

Pünktlichkeit is beyond punctuality.
It is showing up ahead of time for movies,
meetings, and medical appointments;
submitting assignments
safely before deadline;
and returning library books
at least one day before they're due.

Pünktlichkeit is a preemptive way of life,
and not everyone admires it.
Even Rabbi Breuer of Frankfurt,
later of Washington Heights,
scolded guests who rang his doorbell
before the agreed-upon time.
"Zu früh ist auch nicht pünktlich."

But this ethos served my grandparents well.
They left Germany before the *Kristallnacht,*
before the *MS St. Louis,* before their neighbors
were called to trains that went first to France
and then to Auschwitz. Who knows
how many reported to the railways
before the hour they were told?

Birthright

Eyesight dimmed, aged Isaac
could nonetheless discern
the sound of one twin's voice
from the other's
and detect the scent
of each from his garments;

alas, how the story
might have shifted
could the patriarch have distinguished
Esau's skin from a goat's.

Homage to My Skull

after Lucille Clifton's "Homage to My Hips"

Thank God for my skull!
With special thanks to the cranium and its bones frontal, parietal,
occipital, temporal, sphenoid and ethmoid,
without which my brain would long ago have been
jostled and juggled into useless jelly
rather than protected from this fall and that one,
a bump here and there and here again,
and, above all, the assailant's punch and slash across my forehead
that required three dozen stitches
but broke only my cartilaginous nose.
Nourished from the start, if not by mother's milk,
then from fully-functional formula,
and enriched even now by vitamins and *calcium plus D,*
you, Skull, are indeed a crowning glory.

Umbilicus

That late-May morning I was four weeks old,
the firstborn, already
sleeping through the night, my umbilical stump
seeming to have dropped away on schedule,
no colic, no cradle cap. My mother,
confident, drove us to the doctor.

The pediatrician, who had examined me
those first five hospital days, inspected me anew.
Most everything was fine, he said, but this—
he pointed to my navel—must be cauterized,
and he advised my mother
to wait outside.

She was so young that spring of '69,
so she obeyed, and was standing in the hall
when she heard me scream as I had not yet screamed
those four weeks I'd breathed outside her body.
I had to call Dad, she remembers
each time she tells the tale.

My father left his Manhattan office at once
and boarded the subway back to Brooklyn.
By the time he reached us, my screams had stopped.
My mother's sobs continued.
I was far more traumatized than you, she maintains
even now, all these decades later,

but sometimes, when she and I are on the phone,
or in the car, or walking or laughing or worrying
together, just the two of us,
I can't help suspecting that my infant self
understood exactly what it meant to burn that bond.

21

Out to Lunch

When you've been on Weight Watchers for more than a year
and you accompany a group to an old-school soda shoppe,
your eyes bulge when the burger arrives at your booth,
dripping with melted cheese and juices
that simply by sight revive your red blood cells.
And when the waitress sets before you a plate of French fries
so perfectly crisp that they conjure alimentary memories
of even better-looking, better-tasting, oh-so-salty potato sticks,
your stomach cries fat tears of happiness; it gurgles in open joy
when you sip from your neighbor's chocolate malted,
the sweet thickness slithering down your throat.

Kaddish for My Uterus

Exalted and hallowed be Surgery's great name
in the world where none of my gynecologist's earlier ideas—
not the differently-dosed birth control pills,
nor a specific intrauterine device,
nor a D&C—put an end to the mischief
of those four fibroids,
to a daily life constrained by the mess, the pain,
the sheer weariness of endless blood and clots.
May Surgery's majesty be proclaimed
all the remaining days of my lifetime,
joyfully, energetically,
to which I say: *Amen.*

Blessed be Surgery's great name.

Equally blessed, praised, honored, and exalted
be my gynecologist's skill with a scalpel
once she yielded to my entreaties and accepted
that even if I met my soulmate the very next day
I'd long since passed the point
of seeking to preserve my fertility,
such as it may yet have been,
my having already crossed the Rubicon
into my fifth decade
without any concerted effort to make use of it.

May there be abundant gratitude, too,
that I opted for the old-school, traditional approach.
Not for me the ultra-modern robotics,
or the tumor-shredding power morcellator used
in a less invasive laparoscopic procedure
which, while well-intended,
could also send any hidden malignancy shooting through
to stake a fatal claim elsewhere in the body.

23

May the freedom from those four
freakingly frustrating fibroids,
the immeasurable improvement
in my quality of life after Surgery,
bring peace to me, my loved ones, and everyone else
with whom I interact.

To which I say: *Amen.*

This Woman's Prayer

after Esther Raab's "Shirat Ishah" (A Woman's Song)

Blessed be the One
who made me me.
Yes, the One might have aimed higher:
made me smarter, nicer,
more loving, more generous.
But the One could have also have done far less:
given me limitations and burdens
and weaknesses that might have broken me.

Blessed be the One
who made me the daughter of my parents,
who brought me to existence in the United States
in the last third of the twentieth century,
a time after penicillin
and before social media.

Blessed be the One
who made me a reader,
a questioner, a thinker.
Who gave me life and faith
and health and so much—
so infinitely much—
more.

We Are All Bag Ladies

If you're a woman,
  you reach an age when
    you no longer leave the house
      without a bag.

It may be a purse.
  A handbag.
    A clutch.
      A backpack.

Always, something must hold your wallet,
  your keys,
    your phone,
      your lipstick,
        your MetroCard,
        your tampons,
          your tissues,
            your what-have-you.

You forget what it's like
  to venture out beneath the skies
    with your shoulders and back relaxed.

You forget that a person can, in fact,
  walk freely in this world,
    utterly and completely

unencumbered.

September 1, 1946

after W.H. Auden's "September 1, 1939"

Seven years after Auden sat
uncertain and afraid
in one of the dives on 52nd Street,
my great-grandmother arrives, finally, in New York.
She was lucky, everyone will say,
to have left Germany in time,
and to have waited out the war
with her husband in Brazil.

But on September 1, 1946,
she does not feel so lucky.
The endless voyage over, yes;
she is detained on Ellis Island
while her husband, too weak, too tired,
breathes his difficult last in the Marine Hospital;
the unmentionable odor of death
again offends the September night.

On what would have been their fortieth anniversary
she is admitted, alone, to the United States.
For the first time since 1938
she can see and hear and touch her daughter.
They depart South Ferry and make their way
to West 139th Street; there wait
the son-in-law she has yet to meet
and the baby grandson, who will become my father.

Meteorology

For three weeks after the autumnal equinox
the sun still burns strong, the air still steams.
Global warming, we agree. At last comes the day
that dawns dull. Overcast. Walking to work,
or to lunch, we feel the wind nibble,
the atmosphere edge toward the eruption
that comes midafternoon. At five o'clock
a downpour soaks my shoes as I step
into the street on my way to my sister's apartment.
Ten floors above First Avenue, my niece
has abandoned her perch before the television
and stands at the balcony door. Together
we watch the rain pelt the ground and study
the charcoaled sky. She presses her four-year-old palms
against the glass. *Poor Sun,* she says.

A Walker in the Post-Blizzard City

It's like a dream: You can walk
without fear of cars trying to beat the light
or cyclists simply ignoring it.
Pedestrians look straight ahead
instead of down at their phones.
You can walk without needing to weave
between the groups leisurely four abreast
and the double-wide strollers
and, for a time, the evidence
that dogs have preceded you.
For once, it truly is a pleasure
to be a walker in this city,
to tread through the white-blanketed
pathways filled with pure and drifting
not yet driven-over snow.

The Book of Vashti

But Queen Vashti refused to come at the king's command...
The King was greatly incensed, and his fury burned within him.
—Esther 1:12

These silks, and jewels?
He told me to strip them off
and to show myself, naked,
before his friends.

You can only go so long
as obedient servant
when you are a spouse
with pride, and self-worth.

I was cast out,
the royal stage cleared for another
whose name would live on in light
while mine receded.

Until now.

Vocabulary Lesson, 1977

When I was eight years old,
feverish in the camp infirmary
with what would be diagnosed once home
as full-fledged pneumonia,
I was not, shall we say, looking my best:

skin even sallower than usual,
eyeglasses atop my nose,
big buck teeth still a year shy of orthodontia.
I wheezed, and coughed, and tried to keep the thermometer
motionless beneath my tongue.

In the TV room, an older boy surveyed me.
You're homely, he pronounced.

The word was new; the boy could tell.
Do you know what that means? he challenged.
Do you know just how homely you are?

Thus the one who by third grade had become every teacher's pet
discovered that she wasn't so smart, after all.

Ode to a Rescuer

Attention, Nobel Peace Prize committee,
I have a nomination for you:
In Hebron, that volatile place,
a Palestinian one day rescued five Jews.

Five American students from Brooklyn
sought to visit one holy site.
They accidentally strayed from their path,
then encountered some all-too-ready to fight.

Faiz Abu Hamdiah saw the stones and the fire;
he understood the five Jews were in peril.
He ushered them into his home,
giving refuge from crowds going feral.

Then he phoned the Israeli police;
forty minutes passed till they arrived.
Were it not for this rescuer's act,
these five people may not have survived.

That's how everybody should behave,
the savior was quoted as saying.
For a world where such sentiments reign
the rest of us should well be praying.

Jerusalem Dream

In Jerusalem,
>you dream of soldiers, effective
>and tall, protecting the city,
>the streets, and the olive trees.

Suddenly,
>the orderly chain unwinds
>and becomes a Sabbath dance,
>circling over old, flat stones.

The moon is like milk,
>the prayers, like bells.
>Of heaven and God
>you understand the language.

Mannheim

I did not cry the first time I went to Mannheim,
when my father and I studied the nameplates
listing the residents of the building on Ifflenstrasse
where his mother had been born, and grown up.
The building she left one April day in 1938, just in time,

and had never re-entered.
I did not cry even when the current second-floor residents
invited us in, and I stood in the high-ceilinged rooms
where my great-grandparents had withstood the *Kristallnacht*.
In the photos my father snapped
to show my grandmother, back in Brooklyn,
I am smiling.

I did not cry the second time I went to Mannheim,
when my father and mother and sister and I toured the city,
armed with Grandma's handwritten maps,
and visited the shiny blue synagogue.
From the hotel we telephoned Brooklyn
before driving away on the Autobahn.

The third time, the train from Stuttgart stopped.
I descended to the platform.
And the signs read,
Mannheim.
This time my grandmother was gone.
Not just from Germany.
But back in New York her namesake had just arrived.
I blinked a few times. Bit my lip.
Stared at the sign, and swallowed.
Then I walked, fast, through sunbaked streets,
straight to the department store
where I bought the baby a sweater
and tiny socks
before I hurried back to the train station.

Comforts of Home

Jacob left Beer-sheba, and set out for Haran.
—Genesis 28:10

His mother's face.
His father's voice.
Even, maybe, his brother's scent.
And a bowl of lentils.
Perhaps these were the yearnings of Jacob's heart
that lonely night between Beer-sheba and Haran
when he settled his head on its stone pillow
not knowing that the angels awaited
his migratory slumber.

Hypothetical Life

Fresquiennes, a brick and limestone castle outside Rouen in Normandy, is on the market for $2.7 million (2 million euros).

"House Hunting in France,"
NYTimes.com

If I were mistress of Fresquiennes,
rather than my apartment above Third Avenue,
I might buy, or borrow, a horse.

I would learn to ride,
so that I might gallop up the earthen drive
to my castle.

I would marvel at my very own
marble staircase
before entering the library

with its floor-to-ceiling shelves and cabinets
and long rectangular windows that look upon
just some of the 92 acres.

The library, where sunlight streams into the room,
beaming the spirit of Flaubert
upon the oak herringbone parquet.

I would uncork a bottle brought up from
"one of the wine cellars" in the basement
and lift a glass.

Oh, Fresquiennes! To you! To me!
To Flaubert! *L'chaim!*

The First Night

Later—
on what would be their last night together,
till death they did part—
Boaz and Ruth lay in slumber,
each, in parallel,
dreaming back to that first night,
on the threshing floor
beside the grain pile.

He'd been sleeping when she
tiptoed to where he rested,
uncovered his feet
and curled up at his toes.

When he awoke,
startled,
they spoke, first;
then they slid, slowly,
into the space that, unbeknownst to either,
they would share forever
in time, and text,
and story.

On Refinding My First Crush on Facebook

Once Facebook informed me that I'd been tagged
I clicked over to find, straight from 1978,
my third-grade class portrait, the last
before my family's momentous move
to another state. My smile stretched
the length and breadth of decades
as I read my old classmates' comments.
For while some had labeled me *Unknown*
or recalled just my first name (misspelled, still)
it was Anthony,
not once seen or spoken to for thirty-plus years,
who supplied my last name, too.

The O-Word

I see it here, I see it there;
some days, I seem to see it everywhere:
Occupation! so many cry,
never bothering to mention why
or how Israel came to control
certain land and the Western Wall.
Among the critics, too many complain
that all of Israel is occupied terrain.
As if an independent country reigned ere '48.
As if Arabs didn't refuse, in '47, a Palestinian state.
As if, over decades, other offers didn't come.
As if, all this time, Palestinians have abstained from
terror and incitement, murdering and maiming.
As if Israel deserves all—and I mean *all*—of the blaming.
But let's assume that what everyone deplores
concerns only the map post-Six-Day War.
A war Arab provocations forced Israel to begin,
a war the Arab armies never imagined that she'd win.
But win Israel did, and as with elections, it's true:
Wars have consequences, win or lose.
But recall that with Egypt, and Jordan, Israel's leaders agreed
to significant concessions in exchange for peace.
Gaza, Israel exited more than a decade ago—
that's something else many don't seem to know.
So judge the occupation for particularities or duration,
but please don't pin *everything* on the Israeli nation.
It takes more than one to tango and more than one as well
to sustain two states where two peoples can dwell.

Sabbath Rest 2.0

About that Fourth Commandment:
I've always *remembered the Sabbath day;*
I just haven't *kept it holy.*
My Sabbath day is typically tainted—
by writing, say, or boarding a bus or subway.

But these days, I do keep the Sabbath free
from Facebook and Twitter.

And when the sun sinks and sets
and the three stars appear, it's astonishing,
the sense of renewal and refreshment,
the readiness to return once again
to all that awaits my attention.

Bloodlines

My grandmother was remarkably forthcoming
about all matters medical and reproductive.
It is she who introduced me to the words
fibroid and *hysterectomy* decades before
they became my reality as well as hers.
Many times she recounted how the fear of bearing twins
had compelled her to undergo an x-ray
to ensure that she was carrying only
my father, her firstborn, in '44.
She shared not infrequently the ancestral anecdote
of her own father's mother, on a birthing bed
back in Germany, delivering one new life only to hear
the midwife tell her that another was coming.
I don't have money for the first one!
Grandma quoted the new mother weeping through her travail.
But sometime between childbirth and hysterectomy
came something my grandmother spoke of
a little less often, a little more allusively,
something she called *an induced miscarriage*
when she described it to her soon-to-be
daughter-in-law, and, some years later, to me.
We didn't ask for details.
My grandmother is long gone, my father
in his seventies, but I still think, sometimes,
of this younger sibling he never had, this
branch of our family tree that was
broken before it could bloom.
It's not that I'm judging, or can be certain that,
in her place, I'd have done otherwise.
I just wonder what might be different in all of our worlds
if my father weren't an only child.
Who else might be here.
Whom else we might love.

Solar Damage

Beneath thick January clouds I jog
and meet a stranger's eyes. Unimaginable,
that he will punch me in the forehead,
box cutters concealed within his fist.
Thirty-six stitches repair the gash
and newly-dyed-and-styled bangs disguise it.
Laser treatments, I am told, will heal the rest.
That first set of zaps and burns
indeed works wonders, as it should
for five hundred dollars, and it seems that
the scar will disappear with two or three more sessions.
After that, says the specialist, we'll turn to my solar damage.

In the 1970s, in Brooklyn, we children wore sunscreen
only on the hot summer days we spent
splashing in the local pool and
slurping sweet Italian ice by Brighton Beach.
The rest of the time, when not in school,
we played outside, lotionless.
House. Tag. Hopscotch.
Rode bicycles between apartment buildings and
skipped to the sidewalk's edge,
squinting down the street
to glimpse the ice cream trucks
before we heard their bells.

Days, weeks, months of city daylight
before the move to the suburban house,
where I retreated to the attic playroom,
cool basement den or, book in hand,
shady recess sidelines, while
new classmates played games—soccer, softball—
it already seemed late, too late to learn.

I tiptoed back beneath the sun as a teenager,
basting in baby oil beside my best friend.
Both of us intent on roasting
faster, brighter, deeper.
Solar damage there, I concede.
But not from those earlier days.
The new violent scar I will gladly yield.
Not so the solar damage of free freckled youth.

The Smell of Infection

for Dr. Anton Feldman

In the waiting room, I scan Twitter
and see a threaded conversation that hurts my heart.
Lies, damned lies, as some subjects often spark.
At the moment, though, a more urgent pain
pulses in an upper left molar. Hence, this appointment.

With the Novocain injected, my mouth numbed,
the dentist goes to work.
The drill buzzes; an offensive odor fills the air.
That, says the dentist from behind his mask,
is the smell of infection.

About an hour later
the root canals are scraped and scrubbed,
bacteria flushed, decayed tissue removed,
medicine applied, pressure blessedly relieved—
and the stench is gone.

Perhaps, reading Twitter, or Facebook,
some people are too anesthetized to understand—
to discern the lies, the hate, the violence;
to sniff out, in sentence after sentence,
that oh-so-sulfurous smell of infection.

Think how grave the situation, when there is no skilled clinician
no essential scraping or scrubbing:
The bacteria multiply.
The pressure builds.
And the smell of infection worsens.

The Price of Lilith's Freedom

Adam complained before God that the wife He had given him had deserted him, and God sent forth three angels to capture her. They found her in the Red Sea, and they sought to make her go back with the threat that, unless she went, she would lose a hundred of her demon children daily by death. But Lilith preferred this punishment to living with Adam.
—excerpted from Louis Ginzberg, *The Legends of the Jews*
(Volume 1; trans. Henrietta Szold)

The deal was this:
liberation from our unequal coupling
and the ability to spring free from his authority.
In exchange, he gets the house,
where, in time, he'll live with another
and raise a family.
I must travel far, far away.
Each day will bring fresh spasms:
pain, loss, grief—
all to be borne alone.
The deal was this.
And as unbearable as it sounds:
pain, loss, grief—
to be borne,
I repeat,
far away, and alone—
I'd take that deal again.
Any day.

Unsolved Mysteries of Samson and Delilah

Did anyone—
perhaps a prison guard—
ever wonder aloud in Samson's presence:
Dude, what's **wrong** *with you?*

Did anyone point out that Delilah had made it abundantly clear
that she couldn't be trusted?
Did anyone say,
Samson, pal, why on earth did you give her
the power to crush you like that?

And how might the shorn prisoner have responded?
Best sex I've ever had.
I'm a masochist.
I'm a fool.
Maybe
all of the above.

And what about Delilah, anyway?
Did she take all that silver and run,
or did she linger in the neighborhood?
If she dropped by the prison to visit,
did she notice how quickly his hair was growing back?
And was she present the day when Samson
literally brought down that house?

The Autumn of H1N1

It is lucky to live outside the target groups,
fortunate, to be spared chronic disease
and advantageous, to possess an uncompromised
immune system. But something about
the prioritized pregnant women and people
who care for infants under six months of age
unsettles me. Maybe it has to do with that morning
in September, when I telephoned the gynecologist's office
before work. *I'm bleeding,* I said into voicemail.
I've been bleeding all night. Halting—
because who wants to leave this sort of message?
No one called me back. At lunchtime,
still bleeding, still clotting, nearly crying,
I stopped by this doctor's office where I'd had a routine exam
just ten days earlier. As soon as the doctor
came into view, right there in Reception, my composure
cracked. I could barely speak between the sobs.
Calm down, said the doctor, clear enough
for the obviously obstetric patients to hear.
It's not as though you're having a miscarriage.
I know how important mothers are. I cannot imagine
how I will survive when I lose my own. Last year,
I thanked God that a madman chose me to slash
rather than my sister, a single mother to two children, or,
for that matter, my parents, who, since my sister's
separation, have grown older and frailer and even more
essential. Back when my aunt died of lung cancer
at the age of 51, I said that I should have been taken
in her place. I, mired in darkness visible
and dreading each new day, while she struggled to see

another sunrise because she had three children
she could not stand to leave. Mothers
matter. And yet, something troubles about others' decisions—
that my blood counts less, that if somebody
must face illness unvaccinated, it may as well be me.

Ruth's Regret

Once, I'd have done anything for Naomi.
Anything at all.
Willingly.

Wherever you go, I will go;
wherever you lodge, I will lodge;
your people shall be my people;
and your God, my God.

I kept my promises,
didn't I?
I went to Bethlehem
and to the barley fields
and to Boaz.

But no one told me how far this road would go.
No one said that as soon as I bore my baby
the women would carry him away,
chanting a chorus of blessings.
Not on me;
on her.

No one said that milk would leak from me
while my baby nestled at Naomi's breasts.
Even if I loved her with the love of seven sons
(and I'm not saying that I don't)
I'd not relinquish my child.
Not without regret so strong that it paralyzes
and silences me.

Self-Portrait with Root Rescue™

It's expensive, to be a woman
who colors her hair.
It costs money, and time.
(And did I mention that it costs time, and money?)
I indulge in salon visits and try to space them out
as distantly as possible.
Which is how I end up at the drugstore
plucking a box that promises *root rescue* from its shelf,
then returning home to stand before my mirror
applying the freshly mixed chemicals
exactly as the directions instruct:
along the part, the temples, the hairline.
After all these decades on the planet
crows' feet are etched around my eyes.
Age spots overtake the childhood freckles.
And, the toothpaste's assurances aside,
years of coffee and wine have irrevocably stained my teeth.
But along the part, the temples, the hairline,
I've rescued those roots
for just a little longer.

My Mother's Olivetti

My mother was a college sophomore
when she met my dad in '64.
She lived at home, commuted to school.
Tuition was free, but there were fees she paid
through part-time jobs, and her aunts' support.
There was no money for a typewriter.
Three weeks after my parents' first date
came my mother's birthday.
Smitten, my father presented her an Olivetti typewriter.
More than five decades and a series of
electric typewriters, word processors,
computers, tablets, and smartphones later,
that Olivetti, beloved,
remains her prized possession.

Dinah Speaks

They put Hamor and his son Shechem to the sword, took Dinah out of Shechem's house, and went away.

—Genesis 34:26

After my brothers killed my husband and his father
and all the men of my new city; after they took me forth
and claimed everything—and everyone—
that remained for their own,
they returned home with the plundered gold
and farm animals, the women and children
they'd captured, and me.
Our father spoke to them in dismay;
to me, he said nothing.

And here I've passed all the years since.
No more gallivanting.
I stray from my father's tents
only to companion those whom my brothers
seized and spoiled, those whose suffering
surpasses mine by far.
To them alone, I speak.
I am sorry, I say.
I am so very, very sorry.

Family Plots

My mom can tell you stories
about all her mother's sisters.
Except for two. One was stillborn.
Nameless. The other was Shirley.
Shirley, the second to arrive once the family
reunited in New York, my great-grandfather
having immigrated first. Shirley, who died,
the certificate says, on May 7, 1924.
Age: thirteen months.
Cause of death: intestinal toxemia.
It's hard to think of any baby dying,
and hard, too, to imagine Shirley,
buried at once in Mount Zion Cemetery
when her parents and sisters and even
an aunt would be laid to rest together
at Old Montefiore. We visit the graves
at Old Montefiore. We stand gathered
beside them for interments and unveilings.
We recite *Kaddish* at Old Montefiore
and pluck pebbles from its dirt.
We pay for Perpetual Care.
But never—not a single time—
have we visited Mount Zion.
Questioned once, my grandmother,
who was eleven when Shirley died,
recalled the baby's beauty, the frenzy
that surrounded her illness,
my great-grandmother's grief.
But of the cemetery, Grandma said nothing.
Who went there, and when, all the eighty-five years
before I looked up and ordered, for a few dollars,
that copy of the death certificate?

Is it too late, even now,
to move Great-Aunt Shirley to Old Montefiore?
But that might require a visit to Mount Zion,
and I am too afraid of what I'll find there:
the baby buried, alone,
abandoned, with the weeds.

Miriam, Quarantined

So Miriam was shut out of camp seven days;
and the people did not march on until Miriam was readmitted.
—Numbers 12:15

Had another been stricken on the way to the promised land—
had the Divine perhaps punished my brother Aaron
(who, may the record show, was equally at fault)—
I'd have cared for the patient,
no matter how feverish, or contagious, or leprous.

But when *I* was the one afflicted and the Divine refused
my other brother's plea for mercy,
none sat by my side, or brought me water,
or smoothed my brow.

Cast out to suffer seven days in solitude
I knew not what would greet me
once the snow-white scales had faded,
the skin refreshed,
the illness and banishment ended.

How miraculous the discovery:
The people had remained.
How indescribable
the emotions as we set out anew,
together.

Questions for the Critics

Would you be satisfied, then,
if *more* Israelis died?
If children and their parents didn't heed the sirens?
If they didn't burrow beneath the ground?
If the rockets were "better" in design and aim?
If they landed on Ben Yehuda and Dizengoff?
In your calculus, would the Israelis be "justified," then?
Would it all be more "proportionate" (oh, that word!)
if only those hundreds of rockets flying toward them
left fewer able to run, to hide—and to fight back?

The Awakening

Yes, daughter, go, said Naomi.
And so off Ruth went,
out from Bethlehem,
to the fields of barley,
the fields of Boaz.
All that long day Naomi waited,
weak with hunger
and worry.
Had she been younger
or stronger,
she, too, might have gone—
to glean amidst the grain
for bits of kindness.
But Naomi was not young;
she was not strong;
so in Bethlehem she stayed
and slept,
dreaming, sometimes,
of the younger woman,
hidden among the sheaves,
perhaps never to emerge
or return.
With every dream
panic pulsed through Naomi's blood
until she wakened to see before her
Ruth, and food, and
the future.

Sisters, or Double *Chai*

My mother always said:
Be loyal to your sister.
By which she meant:
Do not complain about,
embarrass
or in any other way betray
this person, this younger sibling,
in public.
No matter how much she may
irritate,
disappoint
or perhaps simply confound you,
in word or in deed,
you keep it to yourself.
And if you should hear anyone
criticize this sister of yours,
you must defend her.
You must be loyal.

As I grew older,
my mother's words assumed new significance
and shaped my stance toward Israel.
By which I mean:
I determined I would not complain about,
embarrass
or in any other way betray
this land and its people,
this younger sibling to my American self.
As I heard Others criticize Israel,
my pulse raced, my hands shook
and words leaped up and out.

Like my younger sister,
Israel shares my blood.
I decided to keep any quarrels quiet,
because those outside the family
do not love her as a sister can
and does.

Abel's Brother Anticipates Lady Macbeth:
A Soliloquy

Cain.   What's done cannot be undone.
On another day, in another place,
another man will so write.
But the thought originates with me.
With the evil urge.
I may cry out that my punishment is too much to bear.
I may lament my banishment, my wandering.
I may quake at the thought that anyone who meets me
might then kill me.
But what's done cannot be undone.
Its consequences mitigated, maybe—
with a sevenfold promise and a mark upon my face.
But the deed itself—done.
Now and forever
echoing through time.   *Exit Cain.*

Diaspora: A Prose Poem

Rain delays my flight an hour. Another. Other flights are canceled. Diverted. I wait for my plane to Columbus, Ohio, where the elder daughter of a second cousin will be called to the Torah as a Bat Mitzvah in the morning. I wait, despite the storms and the announcements and the overcrowded Delta terminal in New York and the additional holdup after boarding as thunder rattles the commuter jet on the tarmac, and in the end, I will arrive safely at the Columbus Airport Marriott at two-thirty a.m.

Seven hours later, in the sanctuary of Congregation Tifereth Israel on East Broad Street, young Talia stands behind the Torah. Her maternal grandmother—my father's first cousin—recites a Hebrew prayer in the cadence of the *sabra* she is. The paternal grandparents chant together, with the Lusophone inflections of their family's adopted home in São Paulo, and the entire Brazilian contingent laughs when the rabbi attempts a few words in Portuguese.

And the rest of us—the aunts and uncles and cousins of varying degrees—have converged from Canada and California, from Memphis and Boston, from Raleigh and tiny Williamson, West Virginia, and in our blood and our bones we've reconstructed here the remnants of our common home, the birthplace of my father's parents, and the *sabra*'s, *Deutschland, Deutschland, über alles*. The mid-October sun streams through stained glass into the sanctuary, colors beaming.

Aftermath

These days, it seems that we inhabit
a continuous aftermath.
Each day brings fresh trauma:
an attack, a bombing, a stabbing, a shooting;
sometimes all of the above,
too often multiplied
by five, or ten, or one hundred, or more.
It never ends.
One aftermath bleeds—
literally—into another,
a mournful, discordant,
all-too-chained melody.

Complicity

This happened sometime afterward: Absalom son of David had a beautiful sister named Tamar, and Amnon son of David became infatuated with her.
—II Samuel 13:1

The servant overheard his master, Amnon,
in conversation with a companion.
He knew the plan.

He watched the girl, Tamar,
enter Amnon's home.
He knew the plan.

He obeyed Amnon's command to clear out; he left,
with one lingering glance at the terrified girl.
He knew the plan.

And afterward, when his master Amnon
commanded him to remove
the distraught, disheveled girl;

to send her out into the street
and bolt the door behind her,
he did as he was told

with eyes cast down
and shame squeezing his heart.
Because he'd known the plan.

The End of the Lines

To think of all the bloodstreams that have run into the sea
of this single self, the generations of genes flowing down
through the centuries, combining ever more tightly to form
this discrete skeleton, these limbs, this thinking brain
and beating heart, this centered gravity:
It's breathtaking, and not quite believable.

And sometimes, it saddens me to think that this story will end here,
that the blood I've spilled and secreted, leaked and lost,
will be all that I'll have bequeathed; that, worthy as they are,
words and pages cannot be bound in every way,
cannot pass between bodies, to emerge anew and flow on;
that, on my last day, this river shall run dry.

The Plot of *Madame Bovary* in 55 Words

Girl marries boy she does not love.
Girl reads. A lot.
Girl births baby she does not love.
Girl has affair.
Girl has second affair.
Girl's husband is clueless.
Girl spends too much money.
Girl's husband remains clueless.
Girl is haunted and hunted by creditors.
Girl poisons herself. Dies.
Girl's husband, finally clued-in,
also dies.

Fighting Words

There comes a point, in Deuteronomy,
when I can't help wondering—
is this the match that lights the eternal fire?

The injunctions to *cast them out,*
smite them,
and *utterly destroy them.*

The commands to
make no covenants
and *show no mer*cy.

And just a little later,
the permission, if not
a direct order:

And if it will make no peace with thee,
but will make war against thee,
then thou shalt besiege it.

How much more I prefer those other sacred words
replete with possibility, and hope:
Turn from evil and do good; seek peace, and pursue it.

How much more easily, then,
the word *Amen* springs from my soul
to my mouth.

How vigorously I cling
to the belief that everyone
shares this preference.

Thirteen Ways of Looking at My Latest Cold

after Wallace Stevens's "Thirteen Ways of Looking at a Blackbird"

I

It begins when my sister's baby turns away
while I try to wipe his nose.
He drools against my shoulder.
Sneezes on my arm.
Coughs in my face.

II

You have fish blood! my grandmother used to say
when she clasped my cold, clammy hands.
Today I am feverish.
As I will be for another week.
At least.

III

I cough until I think I will
vomit.

IV

Do not come to be immunized,
reads the staff memo regarding the flu shots,
if you have a moderate or severe illness with a fever.

V

At the drugstore I buy
extra-strength Tylenol,
extra-soft Kleenex,
orange juice, and
cough drops.

VI

You sound like Kathleen Turner,
says the guy who shares my office.

VII

I wouldn't want to stand beside me on the subway
either.

VIII

Maybe it's not "just" a cold.
Maybe the green contents caught within the Kleenex
suggest a sinus infection.

IX

I spend most of the four-day Thanksgiving weekend
sleeping.

X

Maybe I should call the doctor.
Maybe I should take a sick day.

XI

Here's a silver lining:
no guilt for skipping the gym.

XII

God bless FreshDirect
and my father,
both of whom deliver chicken soup
directly to my doorstep.

XIII

Stop complaining!
It's a cold.
At worst,
a sinus infection.
Not cancer.

On Reading Chapter 19 in the Book of Judges

You say that the Bible is just an old book.
But when I consider the story of a Levite's concubine,
I wonder what has changed since those ancient times.

Are there not still women who leave their husbands
only to have the men hunt them down, corner them anew,
refuse to return to the marital home alone?

Are there not still women whose bodies
are handed over to,
then ravaged by gangs of men?

Tell me, please, that no woman has been dismembered
during my own lifetime, and then, maybe,
I can agree that the Bible is just an old book.

Wherever You've Gone, Joe DiMaggio

I turn my eyes, in desperation, to you,
because the current situation is simply too much.
Will anyone say of the nation's 45th president, as was said of you:
He represented the best in America.
It was his character, his generosity, his sensitivity.
He was someone who set a standard every father
would want his children to follow.
Will anyone pronounce him, with sincerity and a straight face,
to be among our *most beloved heroes?*
Who will think of him as someone who
gave every American something to believe in,
representing *the very symbol of American grace, power and skill?*
How many can believe, for even a fractured moment, that
when future generations look back at the best of America
his will be among the faces that surface?

Dayenu

At Passover, we read aloud from the *Haggadah*
and we mention four children.
When I was growing up, we laughed
as each found its match around the table:
the wise child, the rebellious, the simple.
But later, the laughter stopped
when we reached the child who is unable to ask.

We looked at him, this little boy whose brain and muscles
and vocal cords couldn't always communicate.
Back then, we didn't know when he'd be able to ask,
when he might utter intelligible words, let alone questions,
syntactically incorrect as they may still sometimes be.
Now, he sings *Dayenu* with all the other children.
Elijah smiles. Miriam dances. We applaud.

Pharaoh's Daughter Addresses Linda Sarsour

My sister: Zionism is not,
as you have notoriously suggested, "creepy."
I know that you do not believe it.
But if you'd witnessed what I have—
Jews enslaved, their babies murdered—
perhaps you'd understand.

How many generations of Jewish mothers
like the one who birthed my Moses
have feared for their children's safety?
For how many decades, centuries, millennia,
have the Jews lacked a single home of their own
and looked back, with longing, to Zion?

But above and beyond all of that, my sister:
If you believe in self-determination for your own community
how can you deny others the same? I cannot discern
how their aspirations are any "creepier" than yours.
Please, sister, reconsider your past words
and your present ones.

Over the Edge

So far, most of us
are sad, and angry;
disbelieving, and
disheartened.
We post on Facebook
and we tweet;
we make calls
and mail postcards
and wear pink hats.
In the privacy of our homes
we may even scream.
But no one—
at least no one I know of—
has fled this country,
or, as did Walter Benjamin
and Stefan Zweig
and so many less-famous souls,
planned a still more final exit.
What would it take to tip us—
any of us—
over that edge?
What might happen
that could so shatter our souls
and stop our hearts?

Black Sheep in the World to Come

In the world to come
I will see again my grandparents,
and after I have greeted them
I will notice, encircling us,
all of **their** mothers and fathers.
Most of these faces I will recognize,
the eyes and smiles imprinted via photos,
or even earliest childhood memories.
But one man will stand apart and alone,
a decidedly unradiant garment draping him
with more holes than fabric.
To him, I will say:

Allow me to introduce myself.
I am one of your great-grandchildren.
I can't tell you exactly how many you have.
If you were any of my other great-grandfathers
       (and here I will gesture to Kaufmann,
       chatting with the two Jacobs)
I could tell you that and so much more.
But you, well—
you're a different story.

You too, I'll say, turning to the woman
who stands hunched a few feet away.
Her, I will recognize, if only from the unsmiling scan
that my mother's cousin emailed me.
This woman is not Yettie, whose Hebrew name
became mine. She is not Johanna,
wheeled into Maimonides Hospital
to view me through the nursery glass.
Not Hedwig, Kaufmann's first wife,
or Anna, who loved Hedwig's children—
including my father's father—as her own.

75

I know little enough about this great-grandmother.
But I know why she may not be eager to stand beside her husband.

I will address them both:
Shall we begin with your names?
"Joseph"? "Mary"? Really?
And the last name, said to have been bestowed on Ellis Island?
True?

Speaking of Ellis Island:
I've put Ancestry.com to the test,
but since none of us can say
when *either of you came here,*
or even name your country of origin—
"Austria" and "Russia" float interchangeably
from census report to death certificate—
I cannot find the immigration records so easy to trace for others.
For everyone else who lived long enough to make the journey
        (and here I will gesture toward the ancestral clusters)
came here legally,
their voyages recorded in manifests,
their naturalization certificates now in my possession,
even when it meant they had to wait, for years, in other countries
        (here I will glance at Johanna and her Jacob)
or in concentration camps
        (and I will look at Anna).

I will turn again to face them, the parents of my mother's father.
Which brings me to another not-so-sentimental subject.
I refer now to the single story I've heard about you, Joseph.
The only legend passed from your son to his daughter and then
to me. It's been on my mind a lot, amid news and views
of football players beating their wives.
        (Mary's posture will straighten.)

76

Once upon a time, Joseph,
when my mother's father and his brothers were teenagers,
they advanced on you, together,
and warned that if you touched their mother again,
they'd kill you.
They were brawny guys.
My grandfather, who bore a passing resemblance to
Paul Newman, lived to 87 without visiting any doctors,
and his brothers survived him.
You must have believed your boys,
because, I'm told,
you never beat her again.

I will step closer to Mary.
I may reach for her hand as I speak.
I don't know much about your life, either.
Your son, my grandfather,
a divorced dad who saw his children Sundays only,
spoke little of the past.
You had left New York by then.
You never met his daughter, my mother;
you saw my uncle maybe once.
My mother is so close to her cousins on her mother's side
      (and as I allude to their grandchildren,
      Yettie and Jacob will nod)
but she can't even name all those same connections
from her father's.
How and where you died, though,
that I have discovered.
For that much, Ancestry.com—
and a valid credit card—
proved helpful.

Oh, Joseph and Mary,
            (how strange that sounds, still!)
your bloodlines are woven through me just as much
as those of everyone else here.
*And yet **their** photographs are on my mantle,*
***their** stories rest forever in my heart*
in ways that yours never can.
Even Anna—no genetic relation but the woman
my father's father called "Mother" all his life—
is our "Oma" in our scrapbooks and our souls.

I will ask them one last question:
Do you now feel,
in the World to Come,
any regret
for the World that Was?

When Your Niece Attends a Jewish Day School

When your niece attends a Jewish day school,
you're grateful for the security guards who man the lobby desk
and the metal detector installed beside them,
and you obediently fish out your "Relative" ID card
as you enter the building.

When your niece attends a Jewish day school,
you silently bless the nearby precinct headquarters
and actively thank the uniformed officers
who stand at the school's front door
as you arrive for the latest musical,
which, this year, is *Fiddler on the Roof.*

When your niece attends a Jewish day school
and stars as Tevye in that famous play,
you imagine again how much it would have meant
to your refugee grandparents, for whom she is named,
to have met her.

and as the costumed children chant the words to "Anatevka"

you sit, spellbound,
thinking of all the other families assembled with yours
in that first-floor auditorium,
the bonds that connect you,
the ancestral spirits mingling above.

A Single Woman of Valor

A woman of valor, who can find?
—Proverbs 31:10

Far beyond pearls is my value.
After years of self-doubt, and therapy,
my heart at last trusts in me.
I know I lack no fortune.

I repay my good, and, sometimes,
because like one of my beloved grandmothers
I find it difficult to relinquish grudges, my harm.
I seek out wool and linen
(preferably cashmere, and wrinkle-free),
most willingly.

I am like a merchant's ships;
from afar, I bring my sustenance.
I rise while it is still nighttime, and
brew coffee for my household.
I consider and I buy.
I work out.

I sense that my enterprise is good
so I sleep well at night.

I spread out my palm to the poor
and extend my hands to the destitute—
not literally, in most cases,
but more typically via tax-deductible contributions
and GoFundMe campaigns.

I fear not snow for my household,
for I live in a large apartment building
and the city plows clear the streets.

Bedspreads I buy on sale;
Lands' End and TravelSmith are my clothing.

I hope that as I age, smilingly I will await
my last day.

I open my mouth with Wisdom, or so I believe,
and I try, mightily, to remember
my mother's teaching of kindness,
and to keep it on my tongue,
and in my emails.

I anticipate the needs of my household, so that
there is always food, and bottled water, and toilet paper.

I do like the bread of idleness, though—
if by that you mean "naps."

I have no children to rise and celebrate me
and no husband to commend me.

Yet I imagine Solomon himself in agreement that
my deeds may still praise at those gates.

With or Without

Come with me sit with me stay with me play with me lie with me
with all your heart with all your soul with all your might without a
doubt without objection without prejudice without compunction
without exception rebel without a cause man without a country
gone with the wind with the greatest of ease with pleasure with
assistance without really trying without meaning to without a trace
without a care in the world without borders parents without
partners without consent with tears without stopping with a smile
with a laugh with finished basement with washer/dryer with
skylights with bath with salt with fries with dressing on the side
with cheese with tax with fees with honors with distinction with
my compliments with your help with your approval without further
ado let he who is without sin without guile go with God without
parole.

Notes

Steven M. Lowenstein's *Frankfurt on the Hudson: The German-Jewish Community of Washington Heights, 1933-1983* (Wayne State University Press, 1989) provided helpful background for *"Pünktlichkeit,"* including the information about Rabbi Breuer. A literal translation of the line *"Zu früh ist auch nicht pünktlich"* is "Too early is also not on time."

"Birthright" evolved from reflections on Genesis 25 *and* Genesis 27.

"Kaddish for My Uterus" is modeled on the *Kaddish,* known as a Jewish memorial prayer, which notably never mentions death or mourning, but rather focuses on praising God.

Stacy Zisook Robinson's poem "The Book of Esther" inspired my approach to "The Book of Vashti." Both Esther and Vashti appear in Megillat Esther ("The Scroll of Esther"), an account of the events associated with the Jewish holiday of Purim.

In "Ode to a Rescuer," the line "That's how everyone should behave" was reported by Yoav Zitun and Itay Blumenthal on Ynetnews.com ("Palestinian Saves 5 American Tourists from Attack in Hebron," September 4, 2015).

"The First Night," "Ruth's Regret," and "The Awakening" are all inspired by the Book of Ruth.

"Questions for the Critics" was written in response to pervasive discourse that developed alongside what is known in Israel as 2012's Operation Pillar of Defense. It has sadly proved to be an "evergreen" poem and has been reprinted more than once.

"Sisters, or Double *Chai*" invokes the Hebrew meanings of "chai": In Hebrew, "chai" means "life"; it also represents the number 18, as its Hebrew spelling (חי) combines the eighth and tenth letters of the Hebrew alphabet.

The title of "Wherever You've Gone, Joe DiMaggio" is inspired by a line from Simon and Garfunkel's "Mrs. Robinson"; the statements made upon DiMaggio's passing in 1999 (by former New York City Mayor Ed Koch and then-President Bill Clinton) that are quoted were found on Biography.com.

Translated as "it would have been enough," *Dayenu* is the title of a Passover song that expresses gratitude for the multiple miracles that occurred at the time of the Exodus from Egypt; a refrain between stanzas emphasizes that had the Holy One enacted only the preceding miracle, that would have sufficed.

"Pharaoh's Daughter Addresses Linda Sarsour" is a response to pronouncements by activist Sarsour, including a 2012 tweet in which Sarsour stated, "Nothing is creepier than Zionism."

As noted by Aya Baron on the Jewish Women's Archive website (JWA.org), the "Woman of Valor" text *(Eshet chayil)* "is a 22-verse poem found in Proverbs 31, verses 10-31, which delineates qualities of an ideal Jewish woman. This prayer is traditionally read before the *Kiddush* wine blessing as families welcome in *Shabbat* on Friday evening. This is a custom many believe originated with the mystics in Tzfat who connected Shabbat to *shekinah*—the feminine manifestation of The Divine. This prayer has since entered the domestic sphere, with the male head of the home singing it to honor his wife. As such, there are many families for whom this tradition resonates, and many for whom, for a variety of reasons, modern or creative adaptations are a better fit."

About the Author

Born in Brooklyn and raised there and in New Jersey, Erika Dreifus earned undergraduate and graduate degrees, including a PhD in history, from Harvard University, where for several years she taught history, literature, and writing. She is the author of *Quiet Americans: Stories,* which was named an American Library Association/Sophie Brody Medal honor title for outstanding achievement in Jewish literature, a *Jewish Journal* "notable book," and a *Shelf Unbound* "top small-press book." *Birthright* is her first poetry collection. Erika currently lives and writes in New York; her online home is ErikaDreifus.com.